poor tense

poor tense

poor tense

long con verse

Greg Santos

Monterey Road Inc.
Los Angeles, California

Library of Congress Control Number: 2014919753

ISBN-13: 978-0-9908735-1-8

1. American Poetry 2. Art 3. Culture 4. Collections 5. Humor 6. Gambling

First Edition Printed in U.S.A.

jyd

ayting

These are portents; but yet I hope, I hope,
They do not point on me.

– Willy Shakes, Othello

Contents

gentlemen's bet

can't imagine ish
worth half as much
as a two penny poem
scratched on a napkin
by a stranger

keep yer rabid algos
pharma breakthrough ways
mean jack knowhow
architect cultural digests
to yourself

don't you know it too
mr. r.n. d.s. choir
a storied turn on your stake
buys nada time, peace
nor a clue

center cut

it a shit shame trine splain right
around the block
a bout a minute
from the front of your crib
that time you quit waiting
for a late model uber
on a hot corner
a-1 time thing
she'd never forgive
but already forgot
to grab a beer
with the homie calling collect
on account a depression talking
good kid
so over bad coke in the can
every last line meaning less
a modicum of morning
swapped four a.m. shots
back seat burnt trees
heat on blast
in the tha whip
vanilla incense twists
up past the red light
day say uno

mas likely dos
hence the shades
con mis huevos
over mid if mami askin
ain't no question
what remains
died hung, dumb
hand some skinny
bar back a saw buck
to keep it down
wile eye bid adieu
left to lies
indisposed
linking breaths
neath the booth

last resort

summers end
got dem yoots
up in arms
down town cross
beat street strife
way over yonder
in the minor key
minus i d seems
yer tea times
been rain checked
on accounta major
civil under rest
on tha great isle
innit

low end
rocky shores
worse off
sights on signs
of high times
why less use
couch bound
one eye train don
filtered pics
snapped past tense

labelled live
bet u down
like four flats
on a dustcart

dems getting paid
steady streams too
pontificate in pubs
pro grammar stiff
over heel counts
sure as shit
crip walk a rock
through plate glass
night came
daze wuz broke
young and unafraid
dark net say
day pay good
scratch for dat last

so what poe
post crash cubs
deposed todo
but bottle it
wave white rags
wet wit foul
hot piss said parents
find finely suits
as a perfect excuse
for most any atrocity
dare goes
sum bodies
x mas bonus
up in black smoke

keys open doors
bricks beat the rest
cold full bright
night on lock
stretched stick thin
far from chill
durin' dat melee
at last left
thru their own
devices
found a right
to trash
the bloody
lot of it

old folks tripping
untried legs tied
over market woes
heads on hands
stead of steaks
mean time we slept
well fed and high
def made figures
fared best
madoff wit a mint
case you missed it
eyes glued to glass
clocking views
on the tube

three rights

how absurd it all is,
to be sure, hissed the cynic.
eyes glazed over with sherry, halfway
to merry and back.

what a joke! choked
the comic, spitting beer.
tears streaming, cheek to chin,
from the hilarity.

thy will be done,
cried the believer, prostrate.
head bowed heavy, citing ages
of rainfall on stone.

cakewalk

the sweet scent
of miss america
former but forever
remains in the
rented room
shrouded beneath
cool silk sheets
while you lay
giddy as shit
tucked in yer crib
hushed to sleep
by the hiss emitted
from behind
a closed door
green furnished
where there's water
that forever flows
like magic
from gold to stone
an invisible spectrum
in the space between
cold as the wings
of an airplane
else on a whim

blistering on skin
under high sun
a breath away from steam

set back

seen game tricks swept clean
eyes fixed on a point
counted far two soon
four laughs checked tha math
proved low hands weren't worth
co holding

kept well red outta spite
figure father got over
learned hard ways break banks
fool slept on the quick fix
slowplay pitch hit off
the mark

charmed son hardly knew
heard late when he passed
whist her painted miss
known to trump mad fast
tea mate well bent straight
took it

six smudge bet had heart
hope hemming weighs up
pound stakes con papas
dough blaze por shooters

wily chokin' chips wit cold
coke hands

fate graced the table
green felt soft round blocks
housing cats passing gats
priors too, did him in
facing years to pot, still
spent days

pon da same old joke
saint poker god such sums
hearst while even earnest
soul doubt, lost his tapas
hearts watch, the thrown suit
stays paids

over thunk his bid
poor dumb kid got clubbed
sent packing dime thin
caught blind following
so sad state prop locked
up deuce

showin tells mean nothing
on the block, solely
paper make you pay
a ten shun nine ones
forty five verse any face
takes cake

sharp knaves best believe
their bare gun butt pales
to playing the wall
talking capital dub
jack speaks, word up street
tip scales

jet lag

my head's a drum
half full of sand
flung from a train

my brain is a tourist
in a crowded square
counting money

my feet are liars
selfish, dumb
and likely suicidal

my belly's a despot
ruling a nation
of lotus-eaters

what happened

jury's out plus time served
kid caught holding in a bum deal
wit lesson two jacks and a hot piece

cold shouldered straight true
thousand pound dog days
ducking dumb cats with sharp claws

dead end right around the block
in just time gavel came down
case for somebody's good behavior

outside's taxing buddy ain't workin
strong armed into scraping plates to eat
crushed under former representation

promised one promo or another
seems if it ain't broke probly fixed
whiffed when shunned by sumbitches son

baby raised a fuss when they passed him up
plenty steep stares on the street still
better cross broads than hard nails

heard at the well he out on an ear
sis saw him heading south
to say the least of his troubles

old door man tucked an eight
tween the meat crates round the way
back to reaching for a bump to get ahead

gross prospects diminished
two clean holes in a fuel tank
drove home flat out on fumes

worse were the dreams
waking up flush buttered luck
sun so damn tough to swallow

been had cashed his last half stack
net work not worth printing
can't even count on unlisted digits for paper

even he figured it was quits
ten years tempting to smooth out
a rough patch in a bad suit

took a piece to breathing
easy behind a pair of bottles
on the shelf and broken past his prime

found him prone alone at home
back to black never even
split before he ever earned a favor

can't go home again

donate la playa
spoke sea sweet
bronze board shorts
private golf gloved club
public country wide

pros broke out
to white sands
a shred of shame
before the run
drew bank blood

thick blue kingly sums
such mutual misdirection
points toward vacation funds
hid behind long division
minus any work et al.

moving all they got
in stock upstairs
lots underwater
before any odd deal
even ben dunn

drove truckloads
left with less than zero
to funeral masses
each debt passed
stiff as a cinder block

fixed tight
heaved in a lake
spouse's hancock served
shells to remodel the john
before taking a bath

all new modern floor
hardwood laid prior
wall-to-wall baby plans
refine aunts walk-in closet
case uncle comes out

tapped in-laws
whole fam bought it
knowing full well
relative values nothing
like a spare room

i ay

i ay
i ay
ah ye
nay yeezy take it
for himselves cept
his stake mo like given
meanin
aint shit suck seed like success

i ay
i ay
say word
recognize sin, kin
buy nuttin but spit
dat base it, sep interest
meanin
all type a deeds compound

i ay
i ay
may be
back bent least he
pushing paved away
westbound round sunset
meanin
quit, cop a whip n get gone

i ay
i ay
lookin not
tha point of seein
but to be or be out
blind dead by lemonade
meanin
shine son, shine

last ditch

two hard lefts
round about
straight talk
wrong ways
end means
dry old ish
less you own
dem seed rights
bess get used
to starving

oh well fair
ain't got shit
to make do
wit nada
laissez say
it just so
far gone fat
out dough
stretched past
stop limits

high society
wrote off
by the board
accomplice
city of acts
base instinct
point less
whole lot drunk
staggering up
to the right

mean while
nothing grows
don't wither
cept course
interest
debts and bets
forty eight hours
and your tired
ass handed
back

would be

caught a case
of the mundanes
junk bond dropped
a rotten rock
sunk in sand
unloved

coffee gone cold
while holding
course grounds strewn
wit cool beans
getting it by
the pound

if only halle
would pick up
when i call, et al.
stead of screening
favor of sum hot
tech stock

sad lack
of interest
baby turned two
untoward cheeks
sideways smile adding
insult to injury

poles indicate
quite a tight race
but the known known
won first place on a nose
as expected
buy the buy

last deep breath
tough beat breaks
another young heart
spent a good week end
tapping glass
all alone

happy story

we tore a page out
left it in the air
above the grid
locked traffic
way laid up
in the cut
talkin wide open
when
a second stood out
tween sweet repose
barely pale harvest moon
slightly under dressed
through quick silver
wintry breath
a babe roused
out a besotted day dream
cobwebs near cleared
as a stiff broome
wind swept
this very poem
half way across
four thin lanes
in a deep
earthbound arc

stalls, catching
a pair of gasps
coasts east over
iron floats
without flowers
along a sad story
or three
above a bakers
dozen cabs
cuban linked
while a white
stretch limo
hung red beans
long necks crane
rice con a rose
petal trail
sounds off
down town
swore i heard
your name
in a sly whisper
cross the street
but it was just
mary j on blast
from the back
of a glass black
expedition
inching south
like sweat
toward a wedding

call it macaroni

art ain't nuttin
if not some young
monied man's game
post a big, a pac
a clipse split
shit
working beats
got it back word
but who's counting

any sharp made name
gets in line to play
long shots mark hits
so little touché
la vie en bel air
entre mille a day
where roses smell pure
as white hot manure
and dada's monet

first son specs ten x
by summer off spain
spent the whole lot
new moor for the yacht
in mom's name

crowned blue chip prints
who's face fit the frame
pulled proof of a title
before anyone came

thank ice christ
old master rang in
re loaners from london
never supposed to be
labelled fair oh well
moved before finished
better wet than dried up
clients ceiling dropped
sale raised to stay afloat

paddles shout promise
hungry touts circle odds
long on a shameful favor
it girl from elle
even underlings can stand
to gain on the come up
slip their own tips
between sips and cracks
to impress sorry hoes

sum herd espouse status
strong quiet consent
traded semi stable
for an unbridled run
still makes most sense
laying that fit pale filly
fore kings mean this time
last years first place
been broke stone grey

honest living

the gas it takes
to grab a drink
cuts necks
so i hear
saw the charred trailer
before leaving work
least it's steady
warring with dry nuts
they say takes guts
wherein a hood
dare speak
gets one shot
how's that
for an inspired flight
on the early side

but nuttin's easy pop
sun fell behind
as expected
wicked traffic catches
crawling
past a smash
flat broke busloads doze
all day laborers
road it out slow

sleepless on rusted flatbeds
sure skirted a mess
sport flies uptown
lucky stiff
b-lined by the lot
got the last spot

miss thing wished
her gentle man
would a called
blew his shot
copped top stool
held a ticket
straight up
on high, betting
the first one puts out
settled
for a second rate sip
loosened ties
five pockets fat
hearty laughs
for a big tip

two points
never make mates
so all together now
by our lonesome
another, another
well topped cup
appears salty publican
done bought me a few
short minutes more
begs the question
is this all there is?
a running tab
counting on nothing

but olive pits
to mark time

the rest is not our business

awe baby
back a bit
when some
something
or other
wise better day
was here

we laid wet
nights to waste
togged slick
to bricks
pockets out
steaming hot
twenty below

cold chill
bones burnt
weather or not
son showed
on point off center
fresh sans a scent
to spend

less to invest
down jones
so low east
dark side streets
know where
white price
be right

nam mean
vets spittin
yo general derecho
for giggles
sun staring
shit bout
to get heated

den up town
eye ma tell ya
seen your uh
primero cuz
bronx cherry bombs
popping off
sub ways

nine seven
flex n them
doubled up
in the cut
murda music
on the wire
to tap to

rolling deep
else solo
clearly draped
in stank
on ya list
check again
me migo

after horas
fumes fit
the bill sized
split lips
lit kicks
and you say
new york city

whole piece
like whoa when
trade stood still
neg fucks
was a given
swy we took it there
and dim sum